CAMBRIDGE

T0342906

Pre A1 Starters

AUTHENTIC EXAMINATION PAPERS

3

STUDENT'S BOOK

Cambridge University Press
www.cambridge.org/elt

Cambridge Assessment English
www.cambridgeenglish.org

Information on this title: www.cambridge.org/9781108465113

© Cambridge University Press and UCLES 2019

This publication is in copyright. Subject to statutory exception
and to the provisions of relevant collective licensing agreements,
no reproduction of any part may take place without the written
permission of Cambridge University Press & Assessment.

First published 2019

20 19 18 17 16 15 14 13 12 11

Printed in Dubai by Oriental Press

A catalogue record for this publication is available from the British Library

ISBN 978-1-108-46511-3 Student's Book
ISBN 978-1-108-46517-5 Answer Booklet
ISBN 978-1-108-46522-9 Audio CD

The publishers have no responsibility for the persistence or accuracy of URLs
for external or third-party internet websites referred to in this publication, and
do not guarantee that any content on such websites is, or will remain, accurate
or appropriate. Information regarding prices, travel timetables, and other factual
information given in this work is correct at the time of first printing but the
publishers do not guarantee the accuracy of such information thereafter.

Cover illustration: Leo Trinidad/Astound

Contents

Contents

Part 1

– 5 questions –

Listen and draw lines. There is one example.

Mark   Anna   Dan   Sue

Hugo   Grace   Nick

Part 2

– 5 questions –

Read the question. Listen and write a name or a number.
There are two examples.

Examples

What is Jill's new teacher's name?   Mrs .... Long ....

How many children are in Jill's class?   .... 18 ....

Questions

1 What is the name of the school?   .... School

2 Which is Jill's classroom?   ....

3 What is the teacher's favourite song?   ....

4 How many computers are there
    in the classroom?   ....

5 What is the frog's name?   ....

Part 3
– 5 questions –

Listen and tick (✔) the box. There is one example.

Which is Eva's brother?

A ✔   B ☐   C ☐

1   What does Alex want?

A ☐   B ☐   C ☐

2   Where is Ben's tablet?

A ☐   B ☐   C ☐

3 What is Bill's favourite animal?

A ☐ B ☐ C ☐

4 What is Alice doing?

 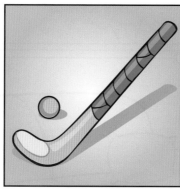 

A ☐ B ☐ C ☐

5 Which is Kim's cat?

A ☐ B ☐ C ☐

Part 4

– 5 questions –

Listen and colour. There is one example.

Reading and Writing

Part 1

– 5 questions –

Look and read. Put a tick (✔) or a cross (✗) in the box.
There are two examples.

Examples

This is a lorry.

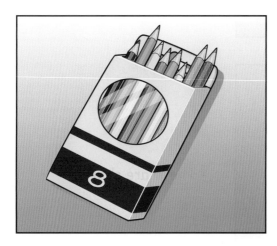

These are pencils.

Questions

1

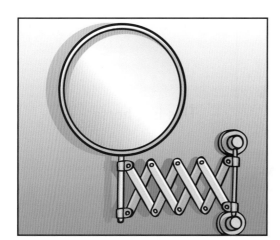

This is a lamp.   ☐

2

This is a balloon. ☐

3

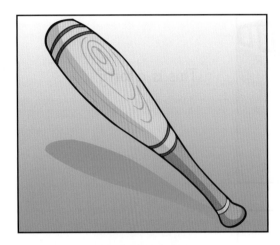

This is a bat. ☐

4

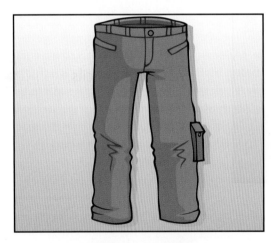

These are shorts. ☐

5

This is a horse. ☐

Part 2

– 5 questions –

Look and read. Write **yes** or **no**.

Examples

A man is swimming.   ....no...................

The woman has got a red bag.   ....yes...................

Questions

1   Some of the children are playing basketball.   ....

2   The dog is sitting next to the boy.   ....

3   There are flowers under the tree.   ....

4   One girl is flying a kite.   ....

5   The birds are standing on the beach.   ....

Part 3
– 5 questions –

Look at the pictures. Look at the letters. Write the words.

Example

<u>b</u> <u>r</u> <u>e</u> <u>a</u> <u>d</u>

Questions

1

_ _ _ _

2

_ _ _ _

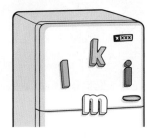

3

_ _ _ _ _ _

4

_ _ _ _ _ _

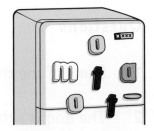

5

_ _ _ _ _ _ _

Part 4
– 5 questions –

Read this. Choose a word from the box. Write the correct word next to numbers 1–5. There is one example.

A donkey

A donkey is an animal. Some donkeys live in the ....ZOO.... . Lots of

donkeys are grey but some are brown. A donkey has two very long

(1) .... on its head. At the end of its body

a donkey has a small **(2)** .... A donkey

can walk and run on its four **(3)** ....

Donkeys drink **(4)** .... They love eating

(5) .... and they like apples, too.

Example

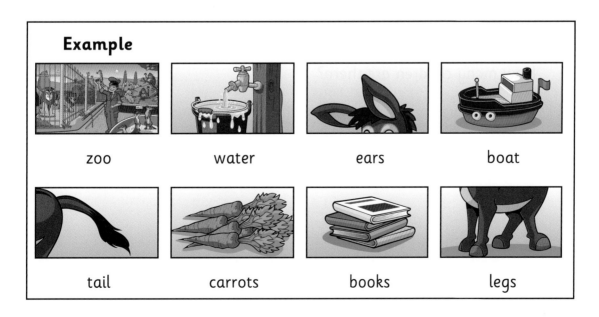

Part 5
– 5 questions –

Look at the pictures and read the questions. Write one-word answers.

Examples

Where is the family?   in the .... garden ....

What is Dad doing?   .... sleeping ....

Questions

1   How many children are there?   ....

2 Where are the children?   in a ....

3 What is on the table?   a ....

4 What is the boy putting on Dad?   a ....

5 Who is taking a photo?   the ....

Blank Page

Part 1

– 5 questions –

Listen and draw lines. There is one example.

Dan   Sam   Alex   Pat

May   Anna   Grace

Part 2
– 5 questions –

**Read the question. Listen and write a name or a number.
There are two examples.**

Examples

What is the name of Kim's dog? ....Ben.....................

How old is Kim's dog? ....1.....................

Questions

1   How many chickens has Kim's mum got?   ....

2   What is the name of Kim's duck?   ....

3   How many goats are in the garden?   ....

4   What is the lizard's name?   ....

5   How old is the lizard?   ....

Part 3
– 5 questions –

Listen and tick (✔) the box. There is one example.

What can the girl's brother do?

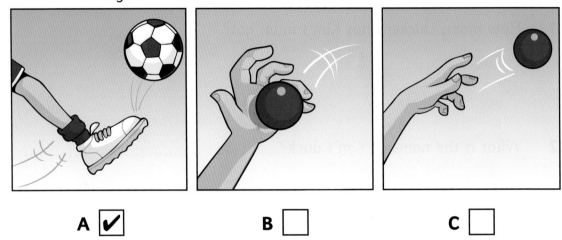

A ✔   B ☐   C ☐

1 What is the teacher giving to the children?

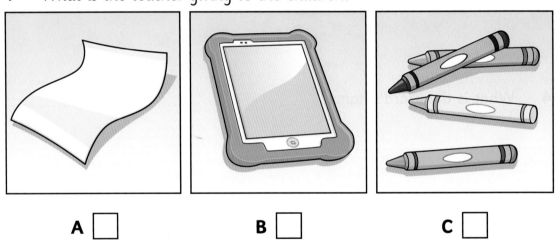

A ☐   B ☐   C ☐

2 Which is Bill's grandma?

A ☐   B ☐   C ☐

3   What would Jill like for lunch?

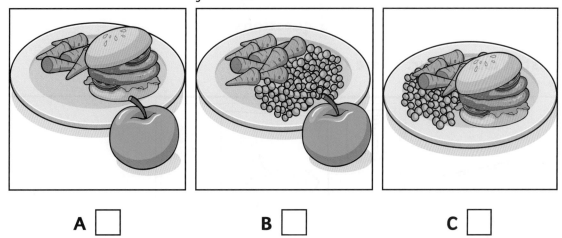

A ☐   B ☐   C ☐

4   Where is Nick's guitar?

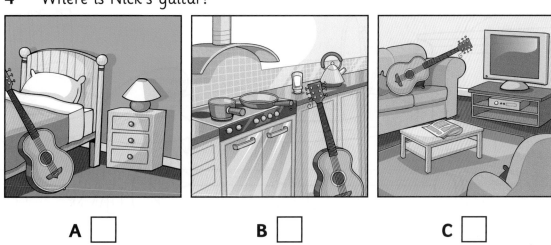

A ☐   B ☐   C ☐

5   What is Eva doing?

A ☐   B ☐   C ☐

Part 4

– 5 questions –

Listen and colour. There is one example.

Reading and Writing

Part 1

– 5 questions –

Look and read. Put a tick (✔) or a cross (✗) in the box.
There are two examples.

Examples

This is a dog.

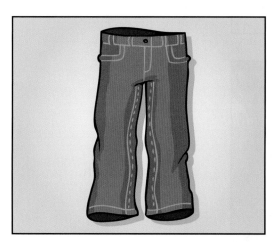

These are shoes.

Questions

1

This is a tablet.

2

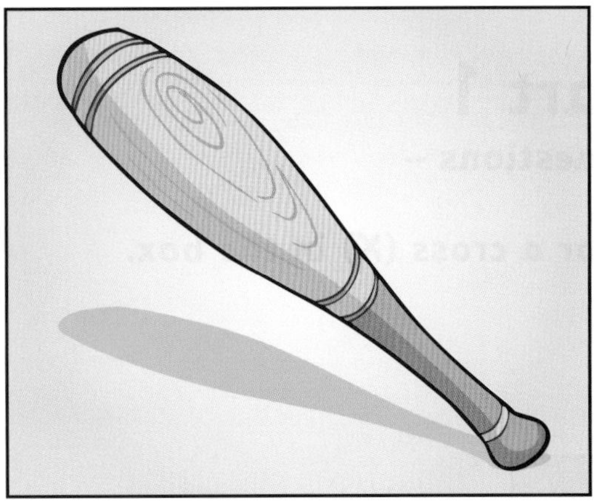

This is a tennis racket. ☐

3

These are bananas. ☐

4

This is a beach. ☐

5

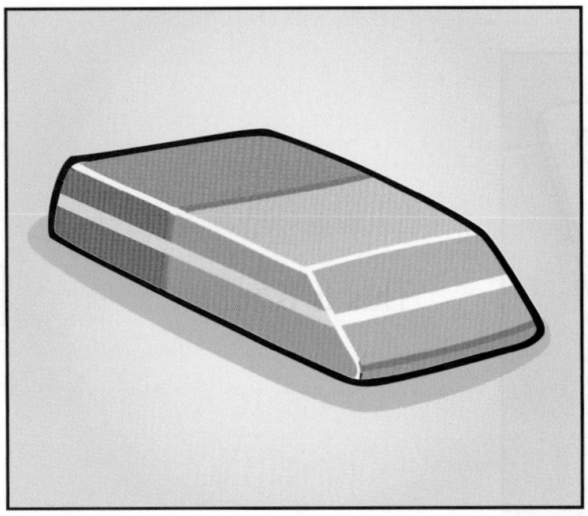

This is a rubber. ☐

Part 2
– 5 questions –

Look and read. Write yes or no.

Examples

One boy is painting a picture of a tree. ....yes................

You can see six children in the garden. ....no...................

Questions

1 One kite is in the tree. ....

2 There are two skateboards. ....

3 One of the girls is wearing a baseball cap. ....

4 You can see the sun. ....

5 Two boys are riding their bikes. ....

Part 3
– 5 questions –

Look at the pictures. Look at the letters. Write the words.

Example

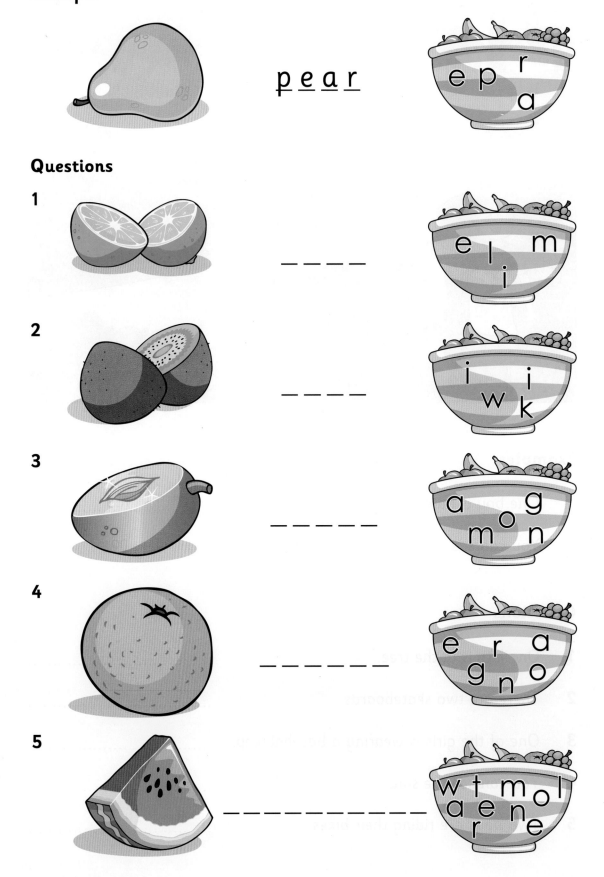

p e a r

Questions

1 _ _ _ _

2 _ _ _ _

3 _ _ _ _ _

4 _ _ _ _ _ _

5 _ _ _ _ _ _ _ _ _

Part 4

– 5 questions –

Read this. Choose a word from the box. Write the correct word next to numbers 1–5. There is one example.

My bedroom

I sleep in a big ....*bed*.... in my bedroom. I've got a desk there, too. I sit

on a **(1)** .... next to my desk. I like doing funny

(2) .... of robots with my crayons. I like reading

(3) .... , too. I've got lots of toys. My favourite toy

is my new **(4)** .... I love music and I'm learning the

(5) .... I play it in my bedroom.

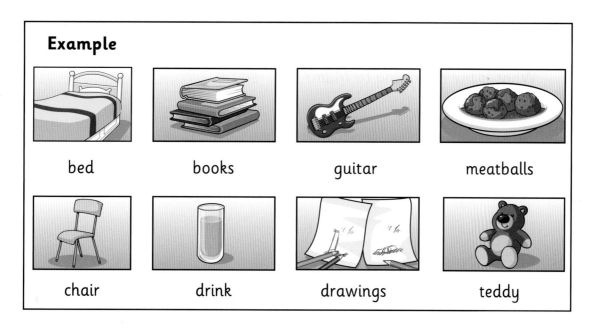

Example

bed	books	guitar	meatballs
chair	drink	drawings	teddy

Part 5
– 5 questions –

Look at the pictures and read the questions. Write one-word answers.

Examples

Where are the family?   in the ....<u>kitchen</u>.........

What is Mum making?   a ....<u>cake</u>.........

Questions

1   What is the girl giving to Mum?   some ....

2   What are the children playing with?   a ....

3   Where is Mum sitting?   on the ....

4   Who's pointing at Dad?   the ....

5   How many ice creams has Dad got?   ....

Blank Page

Part 1
– 5 questions –

Listen and draw lines. There is one example.

Mark   Anna   Ben   Jill

May   Hugo   Sue

Part 2
– 5 questions –

Read the question. Listen and write a name or a number.
There are two examples.

Examples

What is the boy's name? ....Sam..................

How old is he? ....7..................

Questions

1   What is the name of the zoo?   .... Zoo

2   How many monkeys are there in the zoo?   ....

3   What is the name of the funny monkey?   ....

4   What is the name of Sam's teacher?   Mrs ....

5   How many children are there
in Sam's class?   ....

Part 3

– 5 questions –

Listen and tick (✔) the box. There is one example.

Who is in Kim's photo?

A ✔   B ☐   C ☐

1   What animal is Alex thinking about?

A ☐   B ☐   C ☐

2   Which is Grace's monster picture?

A ☐   B ☐   C ☐

3 Where are the tennis rackets?

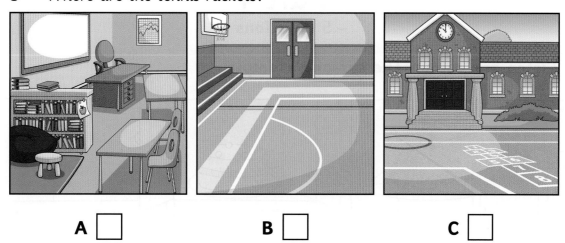

A ☐   B ☐   C ☐

4 What is new in Dan's bedroom?

A ☐   B ☐   C ☐

5 What is in Grandpa's garden?

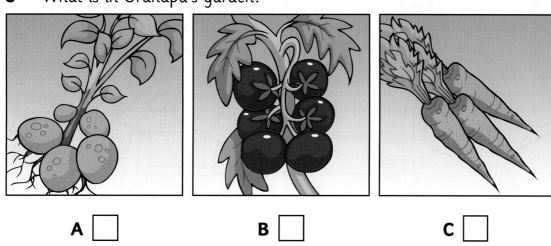

A ☐   B ☐   C ☐

Part 4

– 5 questions –

Listen and colour. There is one example.

Reading and Writing

Part 1
– 5 questions –

Look and read. Put a tick (✔) or a cross (✗) in the box.
There are two examples.

Examples

This is a book.

These are lemons.

Questions

1

This is a bag.

2

These are shirts. ☐

3

This is a radio. ☐

4

These are bats. ☐

5

This is a tree. ☐

Part 2
– 5 questions –

Look and read. Write yes or no.

Examples

A girl is looking at the horse. ....yes.............

There is a bird on the wall. ....no.............

Questions

1 The teacher is cleaning the board. ....

2 The window is open. ....

3 There is a box under the table. ....

4 Two of the children are wearing
red T-shirts. ....

5 The boy with the glasses is looking
at the computer. ....

Part 3

– 5 questions –

Look at the pictures. Look at the letters. Write the words.

Example

 <u>e a r</u>

Questions

1  _ _ _ _

2 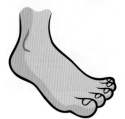 _ _ _ _

3  _ _ _ _

4  _ _ _ _

5  _ _ _ _ _

Part 4
– 5 questions –

Read this. Choose a word from the box. Write the correct word next to numbers 1–5. There is one example.

Tom's cat

Tom's pet is a cat. It lives in the ....*house*.... with Tom and his family.

It has a long tail and two green **(1)** ....

In the morning, the cat plays on the **(2)** ....

on the floor in the living room with Tom. Its favourite toy is a

(3) ....

It drinks its **(4)** .... and eats its

(5) .... in the garden.

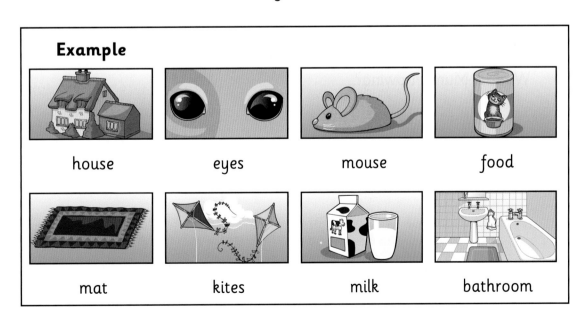

Example			
house	eyes	mouse	food
mat	kites	milk	bathroom

Part 5
– 5 questions –

Look at the pictures and read the questions. Write one-word answers.

Examples

Where are Dad and Grandpa?   in a .... *boat* ....

How many children are there?   .... *two* ....

Questions

1   What is Mum throwing?   a ....

2 What is jumping behind the men?

a ....

3 Who is taking a photo?

the ....

4 How many fish are jumping in the sea now?

....

5 Who is pointing at the fish?

the ....

Blank Page

SCENE PICTURE

Blank Page

OBJECT CARDS

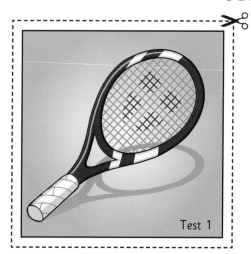

Test 1

Test 1

Test 1

Test 1

Test 1

Test 1

WILDLIFE PAGES

Test 1

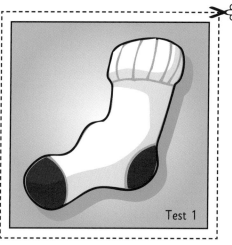

Test 1

Blank Page

SCENE PICTURE

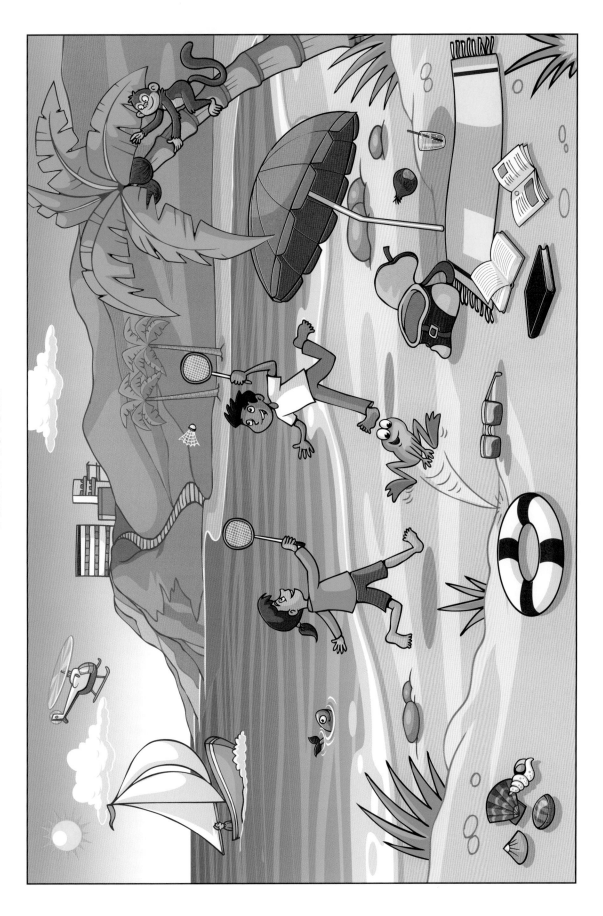

Blank Page

OBJECT CARDS

Test 2

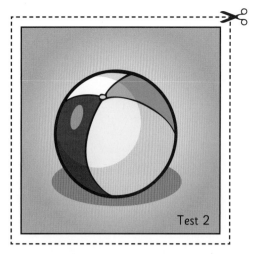

Test 2

Test 2

Test 2

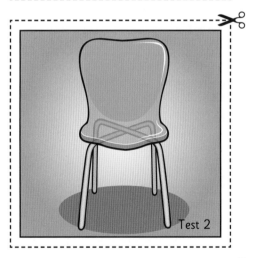

Test 2

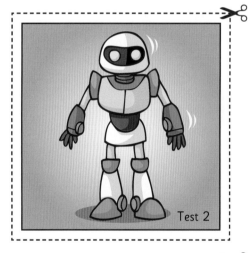

Test 2

Test 2

Test 2

Blank Page

Speaking

SCENE PICTURE

Blank Page

OBJECT CARDS

Test 3

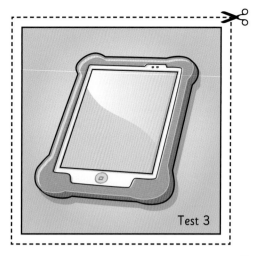

Test 3

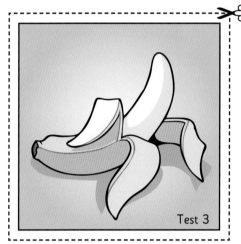

Test 3

Test 3

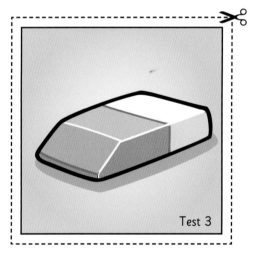

Test 3

Test 3

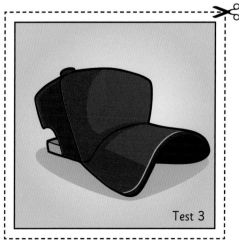

Test 3

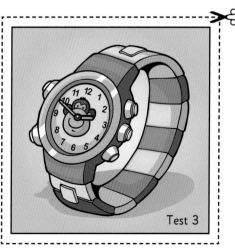

Test 3

Blank Page